FLYING WINGS OF HORTEN BROTHERS

Oranienburg, February 1945: the world's first turbojet-powered flying wing is readied for takeoff.

Hans-Peter DABROWSKI

Schiffer Military/Aviation History
Atglen, PA

Foreword

Doctor Reimar Horten died of heart failure in Villa General Belgrano, Argentina on August 14, 1993. He was the second German to be awarded the "British Gold Medal of Outstanding Achievements in Aeronautics" by the Royal Aeronautical Society of Great Britain (the other was Hugo Ekkener). Sadly this high award did not reach Horten's address until two days after his death. In Argentina, to which he emigrated in 1948, the brilliant aircraft designer and champion of the pure flying wing was able to complete a number of new designs and realize some ambitions which were impossible in Germany during the war and its aftermath.

Towards the end of the Second World War Hitler pinned all his hopes for "final victory" on the so-called "V" and "wonder weapons." In view of the crushing Allied superiority, heavy losses on all fronts, a chaotic supply situation and conflicting areas of responsibility of commanders and offices, it is in fact a miracle that any new developments were completed.

While on the one hand there was a requirement for effective weapons with which to combat the enemy, the serious materials shortage dictated a path which led to simple, cheap and quick production. It is all the more amazing, therefore, that the Horten brothers were able to continue their experimental aircraft program almost until the end of the war. The H IX V2, the world's first jet-powered flying wing and an aircraft far ahead of its time, even managed several flights after February 2, 1945. It was to have been produced in quantity as a fighter under the designation Ho 229. It is noteworthy that every German aircraft maker had a flying wing or at least a tailless design on the drawing board at the end of the war.

The Horten brothers began making a name for themselves in the civilian field in 1933 with the H I all-wing glider. In spite of their structural similarities (e.g. the H IV and H VI to the Ho 229), the Horten gliders will be mentioned only in passing, as will references to aerodynamic problems. These areas have been covered in various books written by competent authors. A complete account of all the Horten flying wings, including complete technical and aerodynamic descriptions of all types to 1960, may be found in the book *Nurflügel* (Weishaupt-Verlag, Graz) compiled by Dr. Reimar Horten and Dipl.-Ing. Peter F. Selinger. The purpose of this effort is to present a general account of Horten aircraft before and during the Second World War and the conditions under which they were created.

Though the following account deals exclusively with the Horten powered aircraft before and during the Second World War, there are two unpowered types that must be mentioned: the H IX V1, a glider version of the later H IX V2 powered aircraft, and the H XIIIa, a research aircraft designed to investigate the low-speed handling characteristics of high-speed all-wing aircraft designed to reach supersonic speeds. The Horten sport gliders will not be mentioned further, so as not to deviate too far from the path from sport glider to jet-powered fighter and futuristic long-range bomber projects, which would exceed the scope of this work.

Photos
Manfred Griehl, Paula van den Hoogen (PH), Gisela Horten, Walter Horten, Horten-Archiv (HA), Volker Koos, Bruno Lange, David Myhra, Heinz J. Nowarra, Peter Petrick, Walter Rösler, Heinz Scheidhauer, Peter F. Selinger, Günter Sengfelder, Reinhold Stadler, Fritz Trenkle, USAF.

Acknowledgements
My heartfelt thanks to those who contributed advice and assistance in realizing this compilation, especially to Heinz Scheidhauer, Edward Uden, Dipl.-Ing. Peter F. Selinger and Dipl.-Ing. Reinhold Stadler.

Translated from the German by David Johnston.

This book was originally published under the title, *Deutsche Nurflügel bis 1945: Die Motor- und Turbinenflugzeuge der Gebrüder Horten,* by Podzun-Pallas Verlag, Wölfersheim-Berstadt, 1995.

Book Design by Robert Biondi.

Copyright © 1995 by Schiffer Publishing Ltd.
Library of Congress Catalog Number: 95-70704

Printed in the United States of America.
ISBN: 0-88740-886-9

We are interested in hearing from authors with book ideas on related topics.

Published by Schiffer Publishing Ltd.
77 Lower Valley Road
Atglen, PA 19310
Please write for a free catalog.
This book may be purchased from the publisher.
Please include $2.95 postage.
Try your bookstore first.

Introduction

From the town of Bonn on the Rhine, brothers Reimar, Walter and Wolfram Horten became involved in model building at an early age in the early nineteen-thirties. Reimar and Walter soon turned to the all-wing configuration. True they did not invent the tailless or all-wing aircraft, but in the course of time their convincing designs attracted new attention to the type. Unlike a conventional aircraft there is no "parasitic" drag from the fuselage. All control functions and every type of useful load, as well as power plants, are accommo-dated inside a correspondingly thick wing. A well-designed all-wing aircraft therefore has less drag and offers a number of performance advantages.

Certain aviation pioneers had investigated or were working on all-wing designs, men such as John William Dunne (England), Hugo Junkers (Germany), John Knydsen Northrop (USA), Alexander Soldenhoff (Switzerland) and Boris Ivanovich Cheranovski (USSR), but generally there was no contact between them. In Germany Alexander Lippisch designed tailless aircraft as the best-known proponent of this idea, but not "pure" all-wing aircraft like those later built by the Horten brothers.

"The German people must become a people of aviators," declared the State Minister of Aviation, Hermann Göring. He said this during peacetime, but surely not without an ulterior motive. In any case sport flying was much promoted in Germany during the 1930's and was extremely popular. Aerobatic aces like Ernst Udet or Gerhard Fieseler had been successful fighter pilots during the First World War and subsequently became film stars. Flying displays were well attended and Around-Germany air races and altitude and range records were celebrated as national events. The outbreak of the Second World War abruptly changed the situation for sport aviation. The Horten brothers joined the Luftwaffe. Reimar joined the gliders in Königsberg and was able to continue his design work. Walter was trained as a bomber pilot, then became a fighter pilot with JG 26 Schlageter (7 kills during the Battle of Britain), was technical officer and finally joined the staff of the General in Command of Fighters. Wolfram became a torpedo-bomber pilot. He was killed in action on May 20, 1940 during an attack in the Bologne area of France.

Alexander Lippisch, Inspiration for the First Horten Flying Wings

Although the Horten designs differed from Lippisch's tailless aircraft in significant areas (Horten used varying distribution of lift without vertical control or stabilizing elements), it was this extraordinary designer who inspired the activities of the brothers. Alexander Lippisch (2/11/1894 – 11/2/1976) began building gliders in 1922 and in 1930 turned to the first tailless designs. Over the course of time hundreds of swept- and delta-wing aircraft sprang from his drawing board, about a third of which were realized. Lippisch was already well-known and respected in sport flying circles by the beginning of the nineteen-thirties.

Following successful testing in 1933 and numerous setbacks in 1934, Reimar and Walter Horten finally received approval for their first manned all-wing glider, the H I with a wingspan of twelve meters. In honor of Lippisch they dubbed it "D-Hangwind" (Upslope Wind), after the gifted professor's nickname. The brothers won the design prize of 600 Reichsmarks in the competition held on the Wasserkuppe in 1934, but the H I could not be saved. There was no way to transport the glider off the mountain and nowhere to store it. Even Lippisch, to whom Reimar Horten gave

Reimar Horten circa 1937. Having previously completed his military service with the Luftwaffe, when war broke out he returned to that service.

Walter Horten (left) in conversation with Professor Ludwig Prandtl, whose positive assessment of the H IIId made it possible for the development of all-wing aircraft to continue during the war years.

the aircraft, was unable to find a tow plane to ferry the glider to the German Research Institute for Gliding Flight (DFS) in Darmstadt. As a result, the H I was broken up and burned on the spot after only seven hours in the air.

Lippisch's best-known design was the Me 163 rocket fighter, which was built by Messerschmitt. On October 2, 1941 Heini Dittmar reached a speed of 1,0003 kph in the A-version, becoming the first man to exceed 1,000 kph in level flight. In 1944 JG 400 was equipped with the operational version, the Me 163 B. Some of these aircraft, dubbed the Kraftei (Power-Egg), flitted through the Allied bomber streams and caused consternation there – victories were few.

Interestingly, in 1945 this Jagdgeschwader was supposed to convert to the jet-powered Ho 229 flying wing fighter – the paths of Lippisch and Horten crossed once again.

The First Powered All-wing Aircraft

The first powered aircraft by the Horten brothers was the H IIm, "D-Habicht." The aircraft was designed as a motorized glider from the outset, in order to avoid the problem of towed takeoffs. Power was provided by a Hirth HM 60 engine driving a two-blade propeller by means of an extension shaft. The undercarriage was a two wheel, single-track design, which proved to be somewhat unstable. The front wheel was retractable and unsprung, the rear rotated about the vertical axis, consequently the aircraft tended to swing to the side. The pilot was accommodated in a prone position.

The aircraft was built "at home" with no official support from the state. With the help of private donations the Habicht (Hawk) was ready in nine months. First flight trials took place in May 1935 at Bonn-Hangelar. As the aircraft still lacked an engine it was necessary to use a winch to get the glider airborne. The brothers subsequently obtained a used but overhauled HM 60 engine and three months later the H IIm was ready to fly again. It proved capable of climbing to 1,000 meters in two and a half minutes and could reach 180 kph in level flight. Once the ignition was switched off the engine could not be restarted in flight.

Pusher propeller of the H IIm "Habicht." (HA)

The H IIm is brought to takeoff position. (HA)

The cockpit glazing in the center-section initially consisted of Mipolan. With exposure to the elements the transparency of this synthetic material soon left something to be desired. However, Dynamit AG of Troisdorf had developed a better material, Astralon, and the company provided some of this for the aircraft.

On account of its docile handling characteristics, the H IIm could be considered well-nigh foolproof. The borrowed engine tended to overheat, but the Horten brothers had a stroke of luck. Hirth loaned them a more powerful 80-H.P. HM 60 R engine for 100 flying hours.

In 1937 the control system of the Habicht was modified to include moveable wingtips. The purpose of the experiment was to demonstrate the advantages of variable dihedral compared to more conventional control surfaces. Unfortunately the aircraft's engine had already been returned to Hirth and a move from Cologne to Berlin was imminent. It was already 1938 and the almost-complete conversion remained unfinished. With the outbreak of war came the ultimate end of the experiment. Nothing is known of the subsequent fate of the H II m.

The H II was followed by the H III, which for all intents and purposes was a larger version of its predecessor with a wingspan of 20.4 meters. The H IIIb, a glider under construction at Bonn-Hangelar, was converted into the H IIId powered glider in 1941/42 and given the code DV+LK. The H IIId was powered by a Walter Mikron engine; situated behind the cockpit, the 55-H.P. power plant drove a fixed-pitch, two-blade propeller directly, without an extension shaft. The aircraft was capable of taking off under its own power. Once initial difficulties with the engine were overcome, the H IIId soon became a popular and much-flown flying wing, although it was considered underpowered.

The H IIId was ferried from Bonn to Göttingen, where it was demonstrated to the director of the Aerodynamics Research Institute (AVA), Professor Ludwig Prandtl on February 27, 1942. Piloting the aircraft was Heinz Scheidhauer. Intrigued by the flawless behavior of the aircraft in flight, Professor Brandtl asked for details of the aircraft and its qualities. His positive report to the RLM ensured that the Horten brothers were able to continue their research through the increasingly difficult war years. The fate of the H IIId is unknown.

As a result of the negative experiences with the Walter Mikron engine in Göttingen, an H IIIb was fit-

The H IIId, which the Horten staff called the "butterfly", wearing German nationality markings.

ted with an air-cooled VW engine and designated the H IIIe, code DV+LL. Driven by five drive belts, an extension shaft turned a self-designed propeller with folding blades; it was a true powered glider and the slimmer engine housing gave the aircraft a more elegant appearance. The maiden flight of the H IIIe took place on January 25, 1944. In 1943 there had been an attempt to convert to movable-wingtip controls, however

D-Habicht in flight (Bonn-Hangelar).

A high-ranking visitor to Göttingen, autumn 1944: Generaloberst Alfred Keller was briefed on the H IIId and saw the aircraft fly.

The completed H IIIe.

The center-section of the H IIIe with VW engine and folding propeller.

this was dropped as a result of technical difficulties. The fate of the H IIIe at the end of the war is unknown.

Oberst Siegfried Knemeyer, RLM Chief of Experimental Aircraft Construction, after a flight in the H IIIe (Göttingen, autumn 1944).

H IIIe in flight.

The First Twin-engined Flying Wing

The first twin-engined flying wing by the Horten brothers was the H Va. Dynamit AG of Troisdorf near Cologne provided support in construction of the prototype which, apart from the engine and undercarriage, was built entirely of a synthetic material. Dynamit was the manufacturer of "Trolitax," the synthetic material used. The D Va provided the company with a suitable test-bed with which to test their product in practice.

The H Va of 1936/37 was preceded in 1935 by the construction of the glider "Hol's der Teufel" (literally "the devil take it"). Though not a flying wing and of

conventional design, the glider's wing structure did make use of synthetic materials. Here and in the building of the flying wings some difficulty was encountered in working with the material. Dynamit AG was able to patent some of the solutions to these problems (bonding and achieving uniform thicknesses and rigidity, for example).

The two pilots were accommodated in prone positions in the nose of the aircraft, which was covered with clear Cellon. The twin-wheel main undercarriage was fixed and both mainwheels were enclosed in fairings, while the nosewheel was retractable. The two counter-rotating Hirth HM 60 R engines drove two-

The H Va, the first flying wing to use synthetic materials in its construction, just prior to its completion in Troisdorf.

Compare the size of the H Va and the H IIm.

blade pusher propellers directly, without resorting to extension shafts. The propellers, which were of an unusual shape, were fabricated by propeller maker Peter Kümpel from Lignol (beech wood impregnated with synthetic resin). Unfortunately there is no information as to their effectiveness. The H Va also had a new type of variable-geometry control system, achieved by using rotating wingtips.

The aircraft's first flight was also its last and took place at Bonn-Hangelar in early 1937. Walter and Reimar Horten were on board the aircraft, which displayed unsatisfactory stability on account of the aft location of the engines. The controls were unable to compensate for the tail-heaviness of the aircraft and the resulting deficit in moment balance on takeoff and the still low speed of the aircraft at that point. The aircraft became airborne briefly then crashed. Luckily there were no serious injuries, apart from Walter Horten's loss of both upper front teeth. On the other hand the aircraft was written off as a total loss on account of the brittle nature of the synthetic material. The only components that could be salvaged were the engines.

Following the crash of the H Va, the brothers built the H Vb in Köln-Ostheim in 1937. Major Dinort instructed the repair facility there to begin construction after the RLM and Ernst Udet gave the green light. It is very likely that the idea of a military (training) aircraft with a free field of fire to the rear (then very popular) was the decisive factor in the approval. In any case this flying wing differed from its unfortunate predecessor in several important ways; construction was "conventional," that is to say of wood and steel tube with fabric covering. The concept of variable-geometry controls was not pursued for this type and the designers returned to the standard arrangement of control surfaces. The pilots were no longer in prone positions, instead sat upright and looked through individual bulged canopies. The nosewheel undercarriage was not retractable but the mainwheels were faired.

The Hirth engines salvaged from the H Va were used to power the aircraft, however they were placed in a more forward location and drove counter-rotating propellers via extension shafts. The much better balanced flying wing made its first flight in the autumn of 1937 at Köln-Ostheim with Walter Horten at the controls.

The H Va prior to its maiden flight . . .

. . . and afterward. The brittle nature of the synthetic material resulted in the complete destruction of the aircraft.

Only the metal-covered engine area survived the crash relatively intact; it was possible to use the engines again.

Horten Aircraft in Difficult Times

The following observations are based to a large extent on the recollections of Reimar Horten; consequently the chronological order does not always correspond to type numbering and vice versa, as planning and realization often overlapped.

Kranich gliders were converted to carry munitions for the planned invasion of England at the Luftwaffe gliding school at Braunschweig-Waggum. Following removal of the duplicate controls and the second seat, the Kranich was able to carry 200 kilograms of munitions. Five Horten III and two Horten II gliders, which were also part of the experimental program, proved capable of carrying 400 kilograms of munitions each with no adverse affect on their good handling qualities. Two incomplete H III gliders had been sitting at Kitzingen airbase since the beginning of the war; in

The H Vb was built in Köln-Ostheim as the successor to the H Va and employed conventional wood/steel tube construction.

Side view of the completed H Vb.

Like its predecessor, the H Vb was equipped with an unusually shaped propeller manufactured by Peter Kümpel.

order to achieve standardization they were to be completed by Peschke and exchanged for the two H II gliders. This was the first military use of Horten aircraft.

As the technical officer of JG 26 Schlageter, Walter Horten often took part in discussions with the General in Command of Fighters in Berlin. At the request of brother Reimar, he told the latter that the H Vb had been sitting out of doors at Potsdam-Werder since the start of the war. If something wasn't done the aircraft – built largely of wood – would soon rot. Walter Horten went to Potsdam personally but at first was unable to do anything about this regrettable situation.

Soon, however, Walter Horten became a member of the staff and the officer responsible for single-seat fighters. He was able to convince Director General of Air Armaments Ernst Udet that it was worthwhile making the H Vb flyable again. Then in September 1941 a special detachment of the Luftwaffe Inspectorate 3 (L In 3) was set up in Minden, Westphalia for the purpose of refurbishing the H Vb. The work was to be done by the firm of Peschke. Otto Peschke was a fighter pilot in the First World War, after which he ran a flying school in Hangelar and finally an aircraft repair business in Minden. Various types were repaired there, such as the Fw 44 Stieglitz,

He 72 Kadett, Fi 156 Storch etc. The Horten brothers and Peschke already knew each other from their time at Hangelar. Reimar Horten became detachment leader and was assigned five men, among them the outstanding pilot and flying wing specialist Heinz Scheidhauer and three designers.

It was now also possible to complete another H III sitting at Bonn-Hangelar. As previously mentioned, it received a Walter Mikron engine and the designation H IIId. Later it became very popular as the "Butterfly," for in this aircraft the pilots had no difficulty at all obtaining the much-desired special ration of food allocated to pilots.

Back to the H V: in Minden the rather weather-beaten two-seater became a single-seater and was assigned the designation H Vc. The aircraft was fitted out as a prototype and the pilot was installed in a normal seated position. The wood-steel tube construction was retained, as were the Hirth engines. As an air force aircraft it received standard camouflage (upper side dark green, bottom side pale blue) and the code PE+HO. The PE stood for Peschke and the HO for Horten – surely not by chance. The first flight took place on May 26, 1942 and Walter Horten subsequently flew the machine to Göttingen.

The H Vc was housed there initially and was occasionally placed at the disposal of the AVA. Flugkapitän Joseph Stüper, a doctor of philosophy and senior lecturer in the service of the state, was then director of the Institute for Experimental Flight Operations and Aviation. In the early summer of 1943 Dr. Stüper carried out calibration flights with the H Vc. One day he took off from the center of the field with the flaps down in the direction of a hangar and was unable to get the machine off the ground in time. The undercarriage grazed the roof of the hangar and the H Vc slid over the roof and fell to the ground on the other side of the building. Stüper escaped with a fright but the flying wing was badly damaged. It was supposed to be rebuilt after the war, but the Allies decided otherwise. Along with other aircraft, the H Vc was burned as part of a "cleanup" action. A projected glider-tug derivative of the H V proceeded no farther than the planning stage.

The H Vc was supposed to be fitted with an Argus-Schmidt pulse jet power plant at the request of the L In 3. Designed by Dipl.-Ing. Paul Schmidt in cooperation with Argus Motoren GmbH, the pulse jet produced 350 kp of thrust. It was of simple design but fuel con-

Above: The extensive glazing of the H Vb with two separate blisters.

Below: The H Vb with landing flaps in the lowered position.

Above: The H Vb ready to take off from Köln-Ostheim airfield.

Right: The completed H Vc. Note the differences from the H Vb.

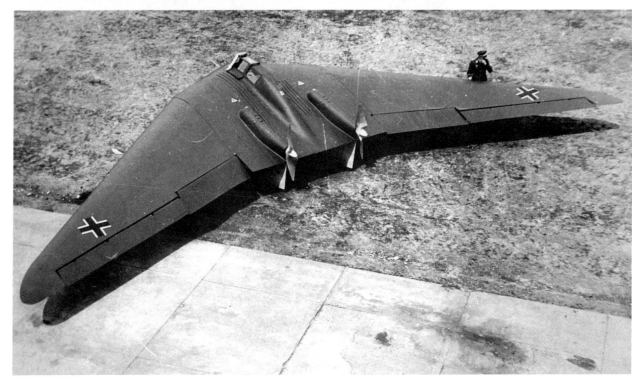

sumption was rather high and the engine was loud and tended to vibrate, which led to installation problems. The tailless design of the H Vc appeared to make it an ideal flying test-bed for the pulse jet. It turned out, however, that a dynamic pressure of at least 1,000 kg/m2 had to be expected and the aircraft was not designed for that. Attention was now turned to a new design, a fully aerobatic two-seater with twin engines. The pulse jet would be installed between the two conventional engines. It was anticipated that the aircraft could be used as a fighter trainer without the pulse jet. The new H VII flying wing was designed in the Göttingen bureau. The wing, of wooden construction, was built in the workshops of the L In 3. Peschke built the center-section of Dural. Two Argus AS 10 C engines drove two-blade propellers with automatic pitch control via extension shafts. The undercarriage was retractable. Aileron functions were supposed to be provided by so called "tongue rudders"; however, these proved ineffective and were replaced by conventional control surfaces. The H VII was a research aircraft with no prospect of quantity production, but for the Peschke company it was an important follow-on contract after it completed refurbishing the H V. Moreover, Reimar Horten was finally going to be allowed to make wind tunnel measurements, which had so far been denied the flying wings.

The aircraft received the RLM number 8-226 (later 8-254) and was flown until February 1945 mostly by Heinz Scheidhauer, Erwin Ziller and Walter Horten. Tests with the Argus-Schmidt engine never took place and the aircraft's sole remaining role was that of fighter trainer. Reichsmarschall Hermann Göring once expressed a desire to see a flight demonstration by a Horten flying wing. His wish was fulfilled at Oranienburg in autumn 1944. Oberst Siegfried Knemeyer, head of testing in the RLM, flew the machine first. Göring was well known as a World War One pilot, but he had taken no part in the subsequent development of gliders and powered designs. Göring insisted on seeing the H VII fly on one engine. Knemeyer, who was on good terms with the Horten brothers, left the demonstration to Heinz Scheidhauer.

The aircraft performed with no impairment of performance. Göring was satisfied and the Peschke firm received an order for the construction of 20 more H VIIs. As well, Peschke laid down three more H IIIs, one of which was fitted with a VW engine as the H IIIe. In the meantime the L In 3 issued orders for the Horten special detachment to be moved to Göttingen and increased in size. Thirty soldiers, drafts-

Below: Walter Horten inspects the completed H Vc flying wing.

men, engineers and craftsmen were assigned to the detachment.

Construction of the H VII V2 began at the end of 1944, however it was never completed. Some components were manufactured for the V3. In February 1944 Heinz Scheidhauer flew the V1 to Göttingen. Hydraulic trouble prevented him from lowering the undercarriage and he was forced to make a belly landing. The damage had not yet been repaired when the airfield was occupied by American troops on April 7, 1945. It is very likely that the H VII also fell victim to a "cleanup" action and was burned.

Initial preparations also began at this time for the design of the H VIII. In autumn 1944 Reichsmarschall Göring's staff office pushed for rival designs for the Junkers Ju 287 jet bomber. The six-engined competitors had to meet the following requirement: deliver a 4,000-kilogram bombload to a target 6,000 kilometers away with a 1,000 kilometer reserve and return. Both Messerschmitt (P. 1108, but with only four jet engines) and Horten (H XVIII) tendered proposals. It was realized that the requirement could not be met with the means available, but the Horten design could theoretically offer approximately 60% greater range than those of Messerschmitt and Junkers. Construction was supposed to begin in Kahla, near Weimar, for chances of receiving a development contract for the long-range bomber of all-wing configuration from the armaments ministry were in fact good.

Though the director of the Aerodynamischen Versuchsanstalt (AVA) Göttingen (Aerodynamic Research Institute), Professor Ludwig Prandtl, was posi-

Side-by-side comparison of the H Vc and the H IV sailplane.

The H Vc, built by Peschke in Minderheide.

tively inclined toward flying wings, he was unable to offer Reimar Horten any hope of using the wind tunnel in the foreseeable future. Use of the wind tunnel was determined by a committee in Berlin, which informed Horten that the tunnel was booked practically "for years." In fact the Horten brothers never got an opportunity to use the wind tunnel before the war came to an end.

In order to keep busy in the interim and begin initial work on the project, the brothers revived the two-year-old H VIII design. With a wingspan of 40 meters, it was almost twice as large as the H III. Six Argus AS 10 engines were to have powered the aircraft. Since

Peschke was set to begin production of the H VII in Minden, there was no difficulty diverting the necessary AS 10 engines with extension shafts. The aircraft's center-section would have been interchangeable with a turbine in order to turn the machine into a flying wind tunnel. The H IX had provided the necessary experience with wooden monocoque construction, so that a ready-to-fly deadline of six months after the start of construction seemed realistic. The aircraft was to provide valuable information for the construction of the H XVIII and later serve as a training aircraft for the long-range bomber.

Walter Horten climbs into the H Vc.

Hermann Göring himself verbally gave the Horten brothers the contract to build the H XVIII on March 12, 1945, without setting any deadline for its completion. It is quite probable that the Reichsmarschall himself did not believe that the aircraft would ever be completed. Nevertheless, work on the H VIII now had a real purpose. In April 1945 American troops discovered the half-built flying wing, which was subsequently scrapped.

One more Horten aircraft from 1944 will be mentioned briefly. It was the H XII, of which little is known. The type was planned as a primary trainer for the H VII fighter trainer. There was no official contract for its construction and so the aircraft was quietly built in the Kitorf branch facility. The intended power plant was a DKW 6-cylinder motor which originally served as an auxiliary power unit in the Heinkel He 177 and which came from a scrapped aircraft of this type. The H XII was built with two seats side-by-side and was flown – still without an engine – at Göttingen by Heinz Scheidhauer at the end of 1944. It is highly unlikely that this flying wing ever flew with its engine installed. The aircraft was destroyed at Göttingen toward the end of the war.

Below: The aircraft taxies out for takeoff. Bottom: The H Vc in flight over the district of Südhannover-Braunschweig.

Opposite and two photos at left: These photos reveal that the registration code PE+HO was applied to the undersurfaces only.

The end of the H Vc in Göttingen. The fire-fighters sprayed the fully-fuelled aircraft with foam as a precaution.

Professor Joseph Stüper (center) once again surveys the crash which he caused.

Above and right: The H VII V1 under construction: note the rearward-retracting double nosewheel and Argus propeller with automatic pitch control.

This propulsion unit with extension shaft and propeller brake belonged to the H VII V2, which was never completed.

Right: Various views of the H VII V1. (HA)

Left: The H VII V1 with extension shaft fairing removed during initial taxying trials in May 1943.

Below: Preparing the H VII V1 for a test flight.

Above: The H VII in flight. It is hard to believe that this flying wing was built 50 years ago.
Below: The aircraft was often seen in Göttingen and Oranienburg, as in this photo. (HA)

Heinz Scheidhauer as a Leutnant in 1943 and (below) with the 4-meter flying model at Nederweert (Holland) in 1993. On the extreme left is the model builder, Erik van den Hoogen; beside him is Aad van Sorgen, who replicated the complicated retractable undercarriage of the original in every detail. (PH)

The original H VII V1 in flight. (HA)

Only a few components of the H VIII were completed before the war ended – here a part of the wing leading edge.

The Path to the Ho 229

The impetus for the design of the H IX came in 1943. In March Walter Horten brought performance curves and installation drawings of the Junkers Jumo 004 turbine engine with him to Göttingen. He had seen the Me 262 at Messerschmitt and subsequently obtained the performance data for the Jumo 004 from Junkers, which at that point were top secret. Walter Horten was aware of the speeds attained by the DFS 194 experimental rocket aircraft and thus the performance that wooden designs were capable of. Work on the H VII immediately ceased and Horten turned its attention to a specification issued by Reichsmarschall Hermann Göring. This called for an aircraft which could carry a 1,000-kilogram bombload to a target 1,000 kilometers away at 1,000 kilometers per hour (hence the name Project 1000x1000x1000). It went so far as to say that no design that failed to meet this target would be accepted. The result was Project H IX. It was presented to Göring's office even though it deviated from the original specification (900 kph, 700 kg bombload, range 2,000 km). Development began nevertheless, and the result was the first jet-powered flying wing to take to the air. The aircraft was originally designed for two BMW 003 turbojets; later, because the BMW engines were not available, it was redesigned for Jumo 004 turbojets. Standard Horten construction methods (wood/steel tube) were used; all skinning was plywood except for metal in the areas near the engines.

Hauptmann Walter Horten managed to obtain a transfer from the staff of the General in Command of Fighters to Göttingen and was thus able to take part in the development of the all-wing jet fighter. On account of his superior rank Walter Horten became detachment commander; brother Reimar, an Oberleutnant, was made his deputy and detachment technical officer. The detachment ceased reporting to

The H IX V1 under construction.

The wings are prepared for shipment.

Above and three opposite: The H IX V1 center-section in Göttingen just prior to transport to the airfield there.

the L In 3 and was renamed "Luftwaffenkommando IX" (Luftwaffe Detachment IX).

Hermann Göring summoned the Horten brothers to Berlin to brief him on the project in August 1943. He subsequently instructed them to complete a single example ready to fly without engines within six months. For inexplicable reasons Luftwaffenkommando IX was disbanded almost simultaneously by Generalfeld-marschall Erhard Milch. Possibly one of the leading aircraft manufacturers was responsible for this measure. Horten reacted immediately by founding the "Horten Flugzeugbau G.m.b.H." and thus saved the Reichsmarschall's project.

The design bureau and part of the workshop had already been working for months on the H IX with all haste and urgency, when news of the detachment's disbandment arrived. To further complicate matters a general decentralization order, intended to make the aircraft industry less vulnerable to air attack, was received at the same time. All work which did not directly involve the H IX was relocated. The high-speed research team went to the State Highway Maintenance Depot in Hersfeld, where 60 men built the H XIII, which incorporated 60 degrees of wing sweepback. The flying group, whose activities were highly visible, was transferred to the Wasserkuppe (Rhön) for reasons of camouflage. Altogether three months were lost to

The trailer carrying the center-section is attached behind a truck and then it's off to Göttingen airfield with a bicycle escort.

The assembled flying wing at Göttingen airfield.

the development of the H IX. After the dispersal actions Kommando IX continued its activities, even though this was not strictly legal. However, the unit was no longer a part of a superior organization and thus lacked a budget. The office of the Reichsmarschall filled all requests as to personnel and materials, but otherwise no longer felt responsible. The Air Ministry had disbanded the detachment, there was no question of that, and the L In 3 had other things to worry about besides the "paper war." A foray into the Luftwaffe personnel office was also unsuccessful. One could therefore say that the H IX (from which came the Ho 229) was developed and built on the highest authority (namely Reichsmarschall Hermann Göring) with the greatest urgency by an organization which did not officially exist, therefore illegally! In the end it was probably fortunate that the work was done without a superior authority, which most likely would have hindered the entire program.

Reimar Horten described the situation at the time as follows: the (unpowered) H IX made its first flight on time, on February 28, 1944, with Heinz Scheidhauer as pilot. The V2 was supposed to fly with jet engines three months later. This deadline was pushed back a full six months thanks to the intervention of the Air Ministry, whose demands and orders as well as omissions interrupted work on the project. At the war's end the confusion was such that even Generalingenieur Lucht resorted to hysterical shouting in an effort to enforce impossible orders; the internal collapse came long before the external one. Ten years had passed since the powered H II had been demonstrated to Herren Antz (officer in charge of special aircraft) and Wendland of the State Air Ministry. The superior qualities and performance of the H IX were the proof that the Air Ministry had wrongly delayed development of the flying wing.

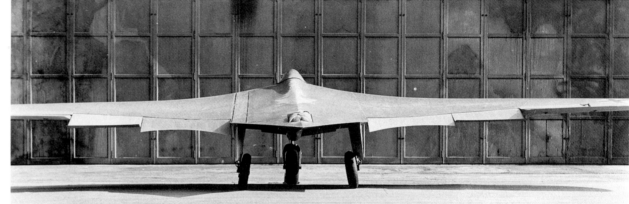

After a number of towed takeoffs Heinz Scheidhauer ferried the aircraft to Oranienburg, where it was tested. The DVL report of April 7, 1944 rated the H IV V1 as a very good gun platform. The mainwheels were faired in order to simulate the stabilizing effect of the missing engines; only the nosewheel was retractable. This collapsed as a result of flutter on Oranienburg's concrete runway on March 5, 1944. Extensive modifications were made to the weak area.

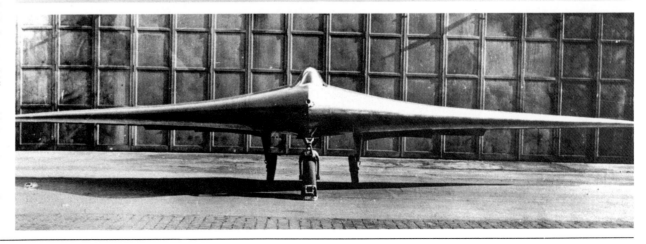

Note the size difference between the H IX and the H IIIe.

Above: The H IX V1 on Göttingen's airfield. The braking chute is stowed in its compartment. Note the wing walkway markings.

No pressurized cockpit was planned for the research glider or subsequent prototypes. A member of the ground personnel dressed in a pressure suit sat in the cockpit to see if the pilot would have the required freedom of movement. This piece of equipment, which resembled a deep-sea diving suit, was found to be of little practical use.

The aircraft was taken to Brandis, where it was tested by the military and where it was to be used for training. Whether the V1 found any use there is not known. The soldiers of the American 9th Armored Division discovered it broken down into major components. It was later burned in one of many "cleanup" actions.

Right: The cockpit of the H IX V1. Subsequent aircraft incorporated a spring-loaded ejection seat intended to allow the pilot to escape the cockpit in an emergency.

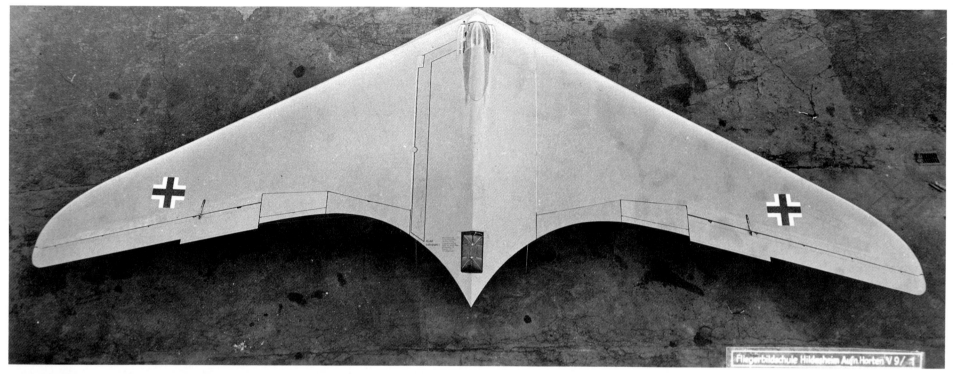

Top: Visible in this overhead view are the arrangement of elevons and flaps and the stowed braking chute; stencilled beside it is the technical information on the type and the narrow walkway leading to the cockpit.

Left: The H IX V1 photographed during a test flight.

A tractor tows the H IX V1 to the takeoff position.

After a test flight. The brake chute has been loosely gathered.

This pressure suit was proposed as an alternative to a pressurized cockpit but was never used.

This page and opposite: February 1944 – the H IX V1 is transported by truck to takeoff position and prepared for a towed takeoff behind a Heinkel 111. There is snow on the ground. Pilot Heinz Scheidhauer climbs into the cockpit. As soon as everything is ready the signal will be given to take off.

The World's First Turbojet-Powered Flying Wing

The second prototype of the H IX was the first turbo-jet-powered flying wing in the world. As a prototype, the aircraft was unarmed. It had a retractable undercarriage and the pilot sat in an upright position. Like the V1, the V2 was of mixed construction. Because of its largely wooden construction the aircraft was difficult for radar to detect and its profile and head-on silhouettes were small – all qualities required of a modern "stealth" fighter.

Difficulties and delays resulted from having to use different power plants than originally planned. The only existing alternative to the BMW 003 turbojet was the Jumo 004; though more powerful, the external diameter of the Junkers engine was greater. Calculations were now out "fore and aft" and the modifications were equivalent to a new design. The aircraft's nosewheel was the tailwheel from a wrecked He 177 bomber complete with retraction mechanism. The main undercarriage members consisted largely of parts from the Bf 109.

The first test flight took place at Oranienburg on February 2, 1945 and lasted about 30 minutes. Pilot was Leutnant Erwin Ziller, a well-known and successful glider pilot whom the Horten brothers knew from the Wasserkuppe. Ziller took part in the attack on the fortress of Eben Emael by glider-borne paratroops on May 10, 1940. In 1941/42 he was director of training with LLG 2 in Parchim and in 1942/43 joined Luftwaffenkommando IX in Göttingen as a test pilot. He was an experienced pilot, with more than 6,000 powered flights at the time testing of the H IX V2 began. Ziller had checked out on the first prototype in December 1944 and January 1945 and flew the turbojet-powered Me 262 a total of five times at Lärz in the period December 29-31, 1944. He was thus somewhat familiar with jet engines but lacked experience.

The second test flight on February 3, 1945 was uneventful, but Ziller released the braking chute too early, resulting in a hard landing. The necessary repairs to the main undercarriage delayed the next test flight until February 18. There was an express order in effect that the aircraft was not to take off without at least one of the Horten brothers present. Weather conditions that day were less than optimal. There is no way of knowing what prompted Leutnant Ziller to take off regardless. The Soviet Army had already

Despite the use of a braking chute, the hangars of Göttingen airfield were dangerously close on landing. Heinz Scheidhauer activates the "emergency brake" – he retracts the nosewheel. The nose of the aircraft drops into the snow and the aircraft stops just in time.

Inflatable air bags are used to carefully put the aircraft back on its feet.

The V1 ended up on its nose again on March 25, 1944; this time the nosewheel collapsed after developing flutter on the concrete runway of Oranienburg airfield. (HA)

This is how American troops discovered the experimental glider in Brandis. It appears that the H IX V1 arrived there but was never assembled.

The H II glider, registration D-10-125, was converted in order to investigate flying characteristics with jet intakes.

Due to the risk of flutter, the nosewheel leg was strengthened by adding a scissors link.

A wing is ready to be mated with the center-section.

reached the Oder and trenches were being dug in Berlin. A desire to help make the aircraft ready for acceptance as quickly as possible may have been the motive for Ziller's actions. After about 45 minutes flight time he dove from great height to within 800 meters of the ground several times, pulling up again on each occasion. He was obviously trying to restart an engine that had failed. At 400 meters the undercarriage came down and the aircraft lost speed. Then there was a howl of turbine noise, the aircraft suddenly entered a right-hand 360-degree turn, nose down with 20 degrees of bank. The machine's speed increased. It made two more full circles at an increasingly steep angle of bank and finally, as it was beginning a fourth 360-degree turn, struck the frozen turf beyond the airfield.

Walter Rösler reached the crash site two and a half minutes after the accident, the first Horten employee to arrive. He later put down his observations in a report. An extract: "The first thing I saw was the two Junkers engines lying on the other side of the railway embankment. I could hear the turbine running down in the still-warm left engine, while there was nothing moving in the cooled-off right engine which lay beside it . . ."

There had been problems with the starboard engine during test runs and the technicians responsible for maintaining it had said that it should actually be replaced. However, replacement was out of the question and they had to make do with what they had. There was a strong smell of fuel at the crash site but no fire broke out on impact. With the exception of the jet engines and the plexiglass canopy, the aircraft was completely destroyed. Ziller was ejected from the aircraft on impact and struck a fruit tree; he was killed instantly. No one knows why he didn't use the radio which had been installed a short time before, why he didn't retract the landing gear and why he tried to reach the field with an engine out. With the close proximity of the engines, the loss of one turbine should not have been a problem. Finally, why he remained in the aircraft in spite of his ejector seat and parachute – in fact he didn't even jettison the canopy – is a mystery. Was he rendered unconscious by carbonizing oil? Was he trying to save the valuable aircraft? The empty com-

Below: The completed steel-tube center-section of the H IX V2.

The tailwheel from an He 177, complete with retraction cylinder and elements of the hydraulics, served as the nosewheel of the V2.

These BMW 003 mock-ups were supposed to be exchanged for the real engines at a later date. (HA)

A Jumo 004 B jet engine on the test bench.

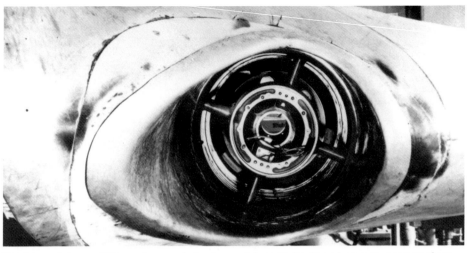

The use of Jumo 004 engines required a number of design changes, among them the use of larger jet intakes.

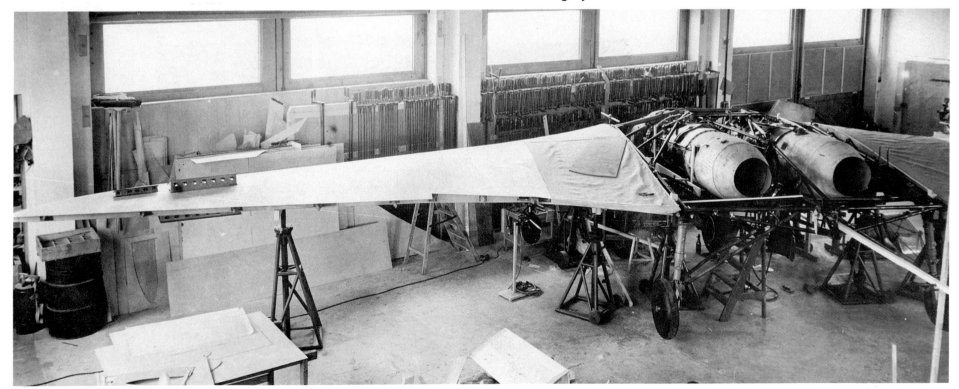

Above and next three pages: Different views of the H IX V2 under construction in a three-car garage of the Göttingen highway maintenance depot, November 1944.

Fliegerbildschule Hildesheim Aufn.Horten IX/70

pressed-air bottle for emergency lowering of the landing gear recovered from the wreck confirmed the loss of an engine and with it the hydraulics. The undercarriage was lowered abruptly, along with the high-drag landing gear doors. A stall or sabotage were not completely eliminated as possible causes. Erwin Ziller would surely have known the answer, but he did not survive the test flight.

Right, below and opposite: The H IX V2 is readied for takeoff at Oranienburg airfield, February 1945.

The only known in-flight photo of the H IX V2, taken in February 1945.

Above: Uffz. Walter Rösler was the first Horten employee to reach the crash site.

Left: Erwin Ziller (right) with comrades shortly after the fall of the Belgian fortress of Eben Emael (11/5/ 1940). Ziller served as a glider pilot and then director of training with LLG 2 (Go 242) at Parchim before he flew the H IX V2. He joined Lw.Kdo.IX in Göttingen in 1942/43. By February 1945 he had made over 6,000 powered flights.

Horten's Last Luftwaffe Flying Wing

By war's end construction of the H IX V3, which like the V2 was powered by two Jumo 004 jet engines and was unarmed, was virtually complete. The aircraft was built by the Gothaer Waggonfabrik (GWF). The power plants were installed splayed 15 degrees left and right of the center-line and inclined 4 degrees nose down, an arrangement tested in a center-section mock-up. On April 14, 1945 members of the American 3rd Army's VIIIth Corps captured the flying wing at Friedrichsrode, to where production of the type had been relocated. The aircraft was later assigned the foreign equipment number T2-490. Additional prototypes were found at Gotha in various stages of construction, but none were nearly so advanced as the V3.

Together with other items of captured equipment the aircraft was taken by ship to the USA and joined

H.H. "Hap" Arnold's collection at the Air Force Technical Museum. The aircraft was supposed to be made flyable in Park Ridge, Illinois, however this plan came to nothing as a result of funding cuts in the late forties and early fifties. Finally the V3 was passed on to what is now the National Air and Space Museum (NASM) in Washington D.C. The aircraft was shipped to Silver Hill in Maryland, where the NASM maintains a branch facility where numerous historic aircraft await restoration. The Ho 229 is still at Silver Hill. Its condition can only be described as pitiful and it is to be hoped that this unique aircraft will be restored in the near future.

Planned Developments

Production of the 8-229 jet-powered flying wing was assigned to the Gothaer Waggonfabrik (GWF). This

aircraft manufacturer had the necessary capacity and, as a result of building various types of glider, the required experience for production. Horten would be able to devote its efforts to further developments. The most commonly used designation was Ho 229 (Ho=Horten), Go 229 (Go=Gotha) less seldom. However, Gotha did continue development of the type, but with its own designers. This resulted in some confusion, as in the case of two different projects designated Ho 229 V6 – one was a two-seater proposed by Horten, the other a completely reworked "Horten-like" single-seater proposed by GWF, which never achieved a concrete shape.

The following paragraphs, which are based largely on official correspondence concerning the 8-229, give some insight into events at that time:

Gotha's provisional technical description of the Ho 229 dated November 22, 1944 anticipated the installation of two Jumo 004 B power plants in the single-

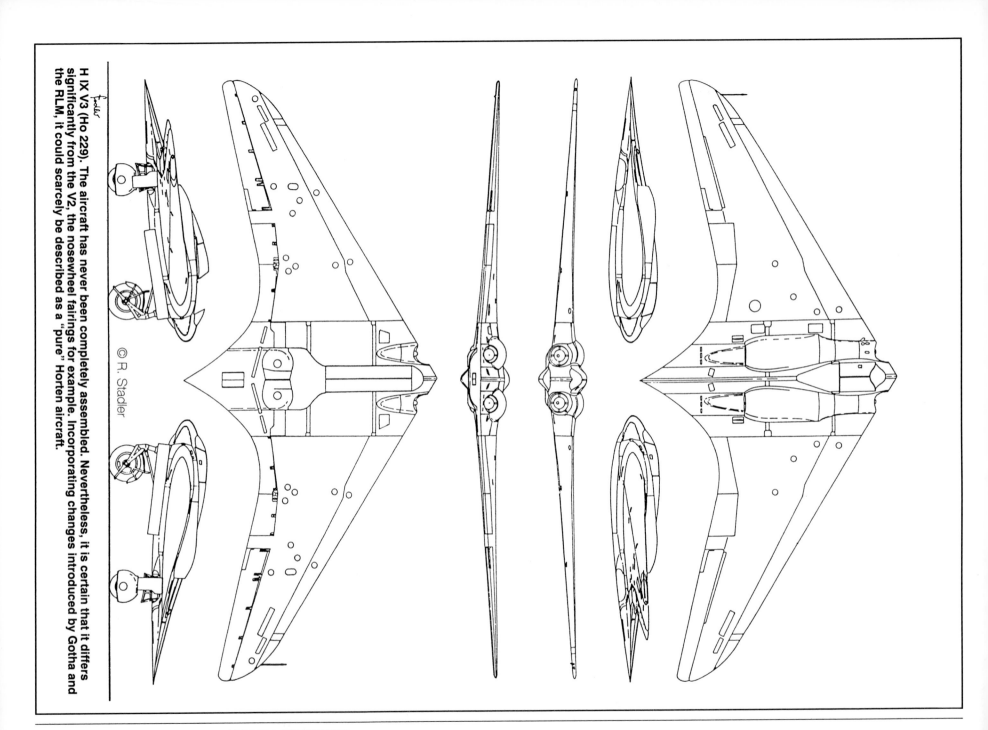

H IX V3 (Ho 229). The aircraft has never been completely assembled. Nevertheless, it is certain that it differs significantly from the V2, the nosewheel fairings for example. Incorporating changes introduced by Gotha and the RLM, it could scarcely be described as a "pure" Horten aircraft.

© R. Stadler

This page and next page: The V3 prior to shipment to the USA.

This is how the Ho 229 was discovered in Friedrichsroda.

It is obvious that further work was done on the center-section. This aircraft escaped the fate suffered by other Horten aircraft – namely destruction.

The Ho 229 in Silver Hill, Maryland, a storage facility of the NASM, in 1982.

Bottom left: The center-section in Friedrichsroda . . .

Bottom right: . . . and today in Silver Hill, Maryland.

seat fighter. It was also supposed to be suitable for use in the fighter-bomber (2-ton bombload) and reconnaissance roles. An ejector seat was provided to permit the pilot to escape the aircraft in an emergency. The undercarriage was retracted hydraulically. Emergency lowering of the undercarriage in the event of a loss of hydraulics (eg. battle damage) was by means of compressed air (2-liter bottle, 150 atm.).

A communication from Gotha to the Technical Office on November 24, 1944 confirmed that the V3, V4 and V5 were to be built as per the "Göttingen model", meaning from Horten plans. Nevertheless, significant changes were planned: the undercarriage, equipment in the cockpit and the ejector seat, relocation of the power plants, and static strengthening of the center-section, wings and control surfaces. The three prototypes were to be unarmed and were intended solely as flight test vehicles with no cameras or other special equipment. Further diverse changes were to be incorporated in the V6 (planned as the prototype for 40 pre-production aircraft) and subsequent aircraft, including a pressurized cockpit "in one of the

next prototypes." Proposed armament consisted of four MK 108 or two MK 103 cannon, both of 30mm caliber. A schräge Musik installation was also planned. The German night fighter force used this system to successfully attack bombers from below, suggesting that the Ho 229 was also being considered for use in that area. An installation consisting of two RB 50/18 cameras mounted at an angle of 7 to 8 degrees was planned for the reconnaissance role.

According to a Gotha communication dated December 15, 1944, an inspection of the V6 mock-up took place at GWF on November 23. Generalingenieur Hermann of the Luftwaffe High Command (OKL) confirmed the redesign of the center-section involving the following modifications: creation of the necessary space for a pressurized cockpit; trouble-free installation of the engines in delivery condition (which was doubtful); good compartmentalization of the engine bays on both sides. Possibility of installing four MK 108 or two MK 103 or two RB 50/18 on one side; improvement of the cockpit canopy.

Gotha designers subsequently introduced the fol-

Left: The instrument panel, virtually intact. Above: 1988, dismantled, probably for the restoration of other German World War II aircraft.

lowing changes into the V6 program: the wing center-section profile was thickened on the bottom side (total maximum 17%) to simplify installation of the engines from the front. As well, the nosewheel was made fully retractable; however, part of the mainwheels still projected. The displacement of the middle rib of the wing center-section forward by ten centimeters and the straight leading edge to the attachment point resulted in a slight leading edge kink. The power plants were moved outboard by 14 centimeters to make room for the pressurized cockpit, but initially only an "armored cockpit" was planned. The nosewheel leg was moved forward 25 centimeters and the retraction mechanism was modified, making more room for the

installation of equipment behind the cockpit. The estimated gross weight of the V6, including armor, MK 108 armament, 400 rounds of ammunition and 2,500 liters of fuel, was 8,127 kilograms.

A Gotha memo dated February 22, 1945 concerning the preliminary inspection of the 8-229 V6 mock-up by Oberleutnant Brüning of the Erprobungsstelle Rechlin stated that several shortcomings remained to be eliminated before the final inspection in Friedrichsroda on March 5, 1945. The problems included an unsatisfactory (too low) seating position for a pilot wearing a parachute and the potential hazard of activating the ejector seat before the canopy was jettisoned. The view through the armored windscreen

had to be improved (to a level near that of the Bf 109 or Fw 190); as well, the emergency canopy jettison handle was difficult for a strapped-in pilot to reach.

Projected developments of the Ho 229 or Go 229 by Gotha never included a two-seater, unlike a Horten proposal for a heavy fighter or bomber-destroyer dated March 1, 1945. The mock-up of the V6 in Friedrichs-roda was virtually complete when a successor to the V3 to V5 prototypes was offered from Göttingen. Essentially, this aircraft was intended to fulfil the same roles as the Gotha one, namely those of fighter (day, night, bad-weather), heavy fighter, light bomber or reconnaissance. Fuel capacity of this V6 was either 1,200 liters in tanks or up to 2,200 liters in the prepared wings.

The prototypes were to use the standard main undercarriage of the Bf 109; later service aircraft would receive the undercarriage of the Me 262, which could accept a gross weight of 11.5 tons. The Horten design also promised the trouble-free installation and removal of the engines from the front, with a choice of

This page and next: Construction of the V4 had begun at Friedrichsroda. This would have been the first aircraft built largely from design plans by Gotha engineers.

BMW 003 or Jumo 004 power plants. Pilot and observer were to sit in an armored pressurized cockpit equipped with ejector seats. in contrast to the Gotha variant, the Horten V6 would have been armed to the teeth: four MK 108 cannon each with 120 rounds, as well as 24 to 36 R4M air-to-air rockets and a Bombenschloss 503 bomb rack under each engine for the carriage of 1,000 kilograms of bombs. Takeoff in this overloaded condition would have required the use of takeoff assist rockets. Estimated gross weights were 8,500 kilograms for the heavy fighter version and 10,500 kilograms for the bomber or reconnaissance version. Planned maximum speed without external loads was 950 kph at ground level.

The two versions of the V 6 ended the Ho 229 series; no further V-numbers are known. A further development by Gotha was assigned Project Number P. 60. However these all-wing aircraft no longer had anything in common with the Horten designs and are to be considered activities designed to keep the company going. A higher priority was certainly placed on the RLM requirements for the installation of weapons and equipment for the night fighter role than was the case with earlier projects. One can also speculate whether Gotha wanted to secure flying-wing development – at least in the area of fighters and heavy fighters – completely for itself and relegate Horten to the construction of experimental aircraft as before.

The Horten brothers did not see the Ho 229 as the ultimate development as far as high-speed, jet-

At war's end the steel-tube center-section of the V5 was also under construction.

powered flying wings were concerned. Their efforts toward supersonic flight began with the design of the H IX. While the H IX was designed for a speed of approximately 950 kph, the H X project went one decisive step farther. After flight tests with delta wing models, construction of a 1:1 scale flying model was begun in 1944. Incorporating 70 degrees of sweepback and a span of 7 meters, the supersonic fighter was to be powered by an He S 011 turbojet and achieve mach 1.4. The pilot occupied a prone position. The aircraft's designers could only speculate on the effects of such speeds on man and materials. With the power plants available in 1945, a suitable aircraft could only have achieved supersonic speeds in a dive. Reimar Horten concluded that the extreme loads could only be endured by a pilot immersed in water and initially projected a water-filled cockpit for the H IX. Because problems were anticipated with conventional control surfaces on account of the limited wingspan and length of only ten meters, Horten deviated from its principle of the pure flying wing without vertical control or stabilizing surfaces for the first time. A ventral fin, which also accommodated the pilot, was planned from the beginning. The 1:1 model was almost complete when US troops arrived in April 1945 and the Horten glider had to be destroyed.

Also to be mentioned in this regard is the H XIII. In 1943 the Bad Hersfeld autobahn maintenance depot was also a center for high-speed research. A glider was built there at that time which had 60 degrees of sweepback and a wingspan of 12 meters. The purpose of the H XIIIa was the investigation of the low-speed characteristics of supersonic all-wing aircraft. The wings from an H IIIb were mated with a newly-designed center-section to produce an aircraft with 60 degrees of sweepback. The pilot was accommodated in a sort of gondola, virtually placing him beneath the wing. Entry to the gondola was from the rear. Visibility from the cockpit was adequate but provision for escape in an emergency was outstanding; after jettisoning the aft section, the pilot had only to let himself drop out of the gondola.

The H XIIIa was flight tested. It made its maiden flight from Göttingen on November 27, 1944 towed by an Hs 126. The pilot of the tug was Oberfeldwebel Knöpfle; in the glider was Hermann Strebel. Following its first flight the H XIIIa was taken to Hornberg, where it was flown approximately 20 times. Towards

An H II (allegedly D-10-125) with engine mock-ups and extended nose as pre-prototype for the H IX V6 two-seater planned by Horten. The conversion offered the pilot an extremely poor view.

the end of the war the aircraft was destroyed by freed prisoners of war.

The H XIIIa marked the beginning of secret preliminary tests as part of the H X project and the designation H XIIIa was assigned to conceal the aircraft's purpose. Following standard procedure, the supersonic project should have been designated H XIIIb or the glider H Xa.

Above: The ready-to-fly research glider was painted in camouflage finish but wore no nationality markings. The figure in the background is part of a poster that was seen everywhere in Germany in those days: "Psst - The enemy is listening!" Below: H XIIIa in flight.

After landing long the aircraft was finally stopped by a fence at the end of the airfield.

Epilogue

Following the Second World War there was no future in sight for aviation, in particular military aviation. Hopes for a continuation of Horten flying wing research were dashed by the victorious powers and in 1948 Reimar Horten emigrated to Argentina. There he was able to realize some of his plans, however a description of his work in Argentina is beyond the scope of this work, as is development work on flying wings in Germany in recent times, which was carried out almost exclusively in cooperation with Reimar Horten.

The Horten brothers began constructing models before they were able to turn to manned designs. In the present day spectacular designs like the Northrop B-2 "Stealth Bomber" attract great public interest — more on account of their immense costs than their unusual configuration. Model aircraft, on the other hand, rarely attract attention outside a circle of enthusiasts. However the same careful and precise calcu-

lations that go into a full-scale aircraft are required in designing a successful model. The slightest error will produce a flying wing with unsatisfactory flight characteristics.

Representative of the many flying wing models, whether original designs or miniature replicas of historic aircraft (which sounds strange given a wingspan of several meters), is a prize-winning radio-controlled aircraft built by Dutchman Erik van den Hoogen. A description of the model will give some idea of the amount of work involved in such a project:

The model represents the H VII V1 and was built with reference to well-known photos. Approximately 1,500 hours of work went into the model, which was built in 1992/93, including 400 hours for the undercarriage alone (fabricated from aluminum by Aad van Sorgen). Scale is 1:4 (wingspan 4 meters) and gross weight 18.4 kilograms. Power is provided by two elec-

tric motors. The wing section matches that of the original and was calculated by Horten specialist Edward Uden. The model is of balsa and plywood construction and is covered with silk. Reimar Horten, with whom Erik van den Hoogen had a good relationship, provided useful tips. Unfortunately he did not live to see the model's maiden flight, although Heinz Scheidhauer, who often flew the original, did. He was able to brief the builder on the characteristics of the design and thus played a major role in replicating the original. Heinz Scheidhauer's brief and telling comment: "Impossible to distinguish from the original" (apart from the dimensions).

And so the "Horten" flew and still flies — in some cases as new designs, in others as radio-controlled replicas of the originals. And as the flying wing will never become the standard, they remain extremely elegant but unusual variations of aviation history.

The H X (H XIIIb) project.

The end of the H XIIIa — destroyed by freed forced laborers.

Brief Summary of Technical Data

Data missing from this summary is not known. Differing figures are possible for projects which existed in several versions. Armaments are those planned.

	Wingspan m	Length m	Height m	Power Plant Type	Output H.P.	Maximum Speed kph	Cruise kph	landing kph	Empty Weight kg	Gross Weight kb	Crew	Armament
H IIm	16.5	5.0	1.65	1 Hirth HM 60 R	80	200	180	49	330	450	1 prone	none
H IIId	20.5	5.0	1.65	1 Walter Mikron	55	160	130	44	300	420	1 sitting	none
H IIIe	20.5	5.0	1.65	1 VW engine	32	140	120	46	340	450	1 sitting	none
H Va	14.0	–	–	2 Hirth HM 60 R	80 H.P. each	280	250	87	1600	1840	2 prone	none
H Vb	16.0	6.0	2.10	2 Hirth HM 60 R	80 H.P. each	260	230	70	1360	1600	2 sitting	none
H Vc	16.0	6.0		2 Hirth HM 60 R	80 H.P. each	260	230	70	1440	1600	1 sitting	none
H VII V1	16.0	7.4	2.6	2 Argus AS 10 C	240 H.P. each	340	310	100	2200	3200	2 sitting	none
H VIII	40.0	13.0	4.4	6 Argus As 10 C	240 H.P. each	280	250	80	5000	8000	3 sitting	none
H IX V1	16.0	6.6	–		–	–	–	75	1900	2000	1 sitting	none
H IX V2	16.76	7.47	2.81	2 Jumo 004 B-2	900 kp each	977†	690†	145†	4844	6776	1 sitting	none
H IX V3	ca. 16.80	7.47	2.81	2 Jumo 004 B-2	900 kp each	977†	632†	156†	5067	7726	1 sitting	none
H IX V4											1 sitting	none
H IX V5											1 sitting	none
H IX V6	ca. 16.8			2 Jumo 004 B-2	900 kp each	950†	630†	144†		8500	2 sitting	4 MK 108 24-36 R4M
H IX V6*	16.75								4965	8127	1 sitting	4 MK 108/2 MK 103
H IX	7.2			1 Jumo 004 B-2	900 kp			88†	600	700	1 prone	none
H XII	16.0			1 DKW 6 cylinder		200	180	75	460	700	2 sitting	none
H XIIIa	12.4	11.28	1.9	–	–	–	–	44	250	330	1 sitting	none
H XVIII	42	19	5.8	6 Jumo 004 B-2	900 kp each	820†	750†	136	11000	32000	3 sitting	

* = Gotha version, † = estimated

Bibliography

R. Horten/P.F. Selinger: *Nurflügel*, Weishaupt-Verlag, Graz 1983

D. Myhra: *Horten 229*, Monogram Close Up No. 12, Boylston 1983

B. Lange: *Typenbuch der deutschen Luftfahrttechnik*, Bernard & Graefe Verlag, Koblenz 1986

A. Lippisch: *Erinnerungen*, Luftfahrtverlag Axel Zuerl, Steinebach-Wörthsee, ca 1977

A. Lippisch: *Ein Dreieck fliegt*, Motorbuch Verlag, Stuttgart 1976

T-2 Report German Flying Wings Designed by Horten Brothers, Wright Patterson AFB 1946

W. Rösler: Bericht über den Flugunfall des Turbinen-Nurflügel-Flugzeuges Horten IX V2 . . ., 1985, unpublished

Working discussion on the 229 mock-up, Gotha, 13/10/1944

DVL report on the flying characteristics of the Horten H IX V1, Berlin-Adlershof, July 7, 1944

Engine installation in Go 229 (Horten) (V3 + V5), Junkers Flugzeug- und Motorenwerke A.G., March 7, 1945

Log book Lt. Erwin Ziller via Dr. Jörg Ziller

H.P. Dabrowski: *Nurflügel: Die Ho 229 – Vorläufer der heutigen B 2*, Podzun-Pallas Verlag, Friedberg 1990

Flug- und Modelltechnik, Issue 453: FMT-Inter-EX and Nachruf Dr. Reimar Horten by Edward uden, October 1993

Aerokurier 3/1994: Lebensinhalt Nurflügel by P.F. Selinger and PUL-10: Hortens letzter Entwurf by Heiko Müller

Yearbook of the DGLR 1993/II: Horten H IX, der Nurflügel aus Göttingen by R. Stadler

Photos
Manfred Griehl, Paula van den Hoogen (PH), Gisela Horten, Walter Horten, Horten-Archiv (HA), Volker Koos, Bruno Lange, David Myhra, Heinz J. Nowarra, Peter Petrick, Walter Rösler, Heinz Scheidhauer, Peter F. Selinger, Günter Sengfelder, Reinhold Stadler, Fritz Trenkle, USAF.

Acknowledgements
My heartfelt thanks to those who contributed advice and assistance in realizing this compilation, especially to Heinz Scheidhauer, Edward Uden, Dipl.-Ing. Peter F. Selinger and Dipl.-Ing. Reinhold Stadler.